What is sight?

Molly Aloian

🌱 Crabtree Publishing Company

www.crabtreebooks.com

Author
Molly Aloian

Publishing plan research and development
Sean Charlebois, Reagan Miller
Crabtree Publishing Company

Editorial director
Kathy Middleton

Editor
Crystal Sikkens

Proofreader
Kelley McNiven

Design
Samara Parent

Photo research
Samara Parent

Production coordinator
and prepress technician
Samara Parent

Print coordinator
Katherine Berti

Photographs
Thinkstock: cover (center), pages 9, 11, 12 (right), 19, 21
Wikimedia Commons: Ataturk.svg: Nevit: cover (right center),
   page 13
All other images by Shutterstock

Library and Archives Canada Cataloguing in Publication

Aloian, Molly
    What is sight? / Molly Aloian.

(Senses close-up)
Includes index.
Issued also in electronic format.
ISBN 978-0-7787-0969-5 (bound).--ISBN 978-0-7787-0996-1 (pbk.)

    1. Vision--Juvenile literature. I. Title. II. Series: Senses close-up

QP475.7.A56 2013   j612.8'4   C2013-901614-7

Library of Congress Cataloging-in-Publication Data

Aloian, Molly.
    What is sight? / Molly Aloian.
        pages cm. -- (Senses close-up)
    Audience: 5-8.
    Audience: K to grade 3.
    Includes index.
    ISBN 978-0-7787-0969-5 (reinforced library binding) -- ISBN 978-0-7787-
0996-1 (pbk.) -- ISBN 978-1-4271-9291-2 (electronic pdf) -- ISBN 978-1-4271-
9215-8 (electronic html)
    1. Vision--Juvenile literature. 2. Eye--Juvenile literature. I. Title.

QP475.7.A33 2013
612.8'4--dc23
                                        2013009067

Crabtree Publishing Company

www.crabtreebooks.com   1-800-387-7650

Printed in the U.S.A./042013/SX20130306

Published in Canada
Crabtree Publishing
616 Welland Ave.
St. Catharines, Ontario
L2M 5V6

Published in the United States
Crabtree Publishing
PMB 59051
350 Fifth Avenue, 59th Floor
New York, New York 10118

Published in the United Kingdom
Crabtree Publishing
Maritime House
Basin Road North, Hove
BN41 1WR

Published in Australia
Crabtree Publishing
3 Charles Street
Coburg North
VIC 3058

Contents

Your sense of sight 4

Eye spy 6

Parts of the eye.........................8

Light in your eyes 10

Right to the retina 12

Lights out 14

Animals see, too 16

Help to see 18

Protect your eyes 20

See and draw 22

Learning more............23

Words to know
and Index 24

Your sense of sight

Sight is one of your five main senses. Your other four senses are touch, hearing, taste, and smell. You find out about the world around you by using your senses. Your senses help you discover what kinds of foods you like to eat, what music you like to listen to, and what kind of flowers are your favorite. Your senses also help to keep you safe.

Seeing the sights

Your sense of sight allows you to see what is going on around you. Stop for a moment and take a look around. What do you see?

Your sense of sight helps you stay out of the way of cars, trains, and buses that are speeding by.

Eye spy

Your sense of sight allows you to see many things. You can see things that are close up and you can see things that are far away. You can see many colors and textures. You can see different shapes and sizes.

Familiar faces

Your sense of sight also lets you see familiar faces such as your mother, father, brother, and sister. You can also recognize the faces of your friends.

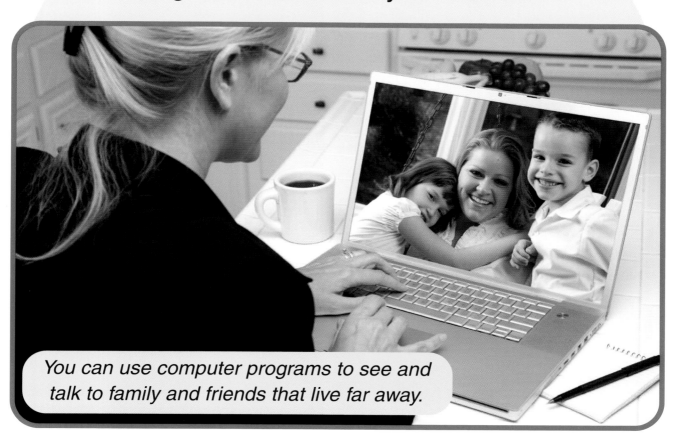

You can use computer programs to see and talk to family and friends that live far away.

Parts of the eye

Your eyes have many different parts. The **cornea** is a clear covering over each eye. It covers the **iris** and **pupil**. The iris is the colored part of your eye. The pupil is the round, black opening in the middle of each eye. There is also a lens behind the pupil and a **retina** at the back of each eye.

Your eyelids, eyelashes, and eyebrows all help to keep things out of your eyes.

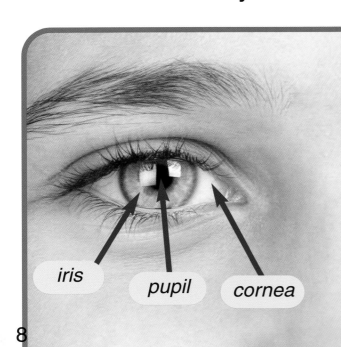

iris

pupil

cornea

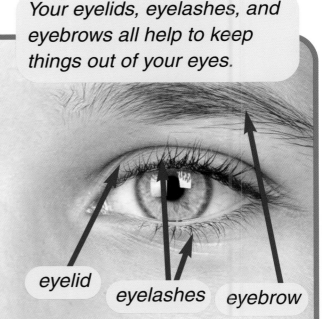

eyelid

eyelashes

eyebrow

8

Look in a mirror and take a close look at your eyes. What color are your irises? Can you see your pupils? Look at your friend's eyes, are they the same as yours?

Light in your eyes

When you look at something, light bounces off of the object and goes into your eyes. First, the light travels through the cornea.
It then goes through your pupils and into the **lenses**.

What do you think?

If you close or cover your eyes with a blindfold, you cannot see. Why do you think this is?

10

Lenses shine light

The lenses bend the light, making the things you see sharp and clear. They focus on things that are close up and far away. The lenses shine the light onto the retina at the back of each eye.

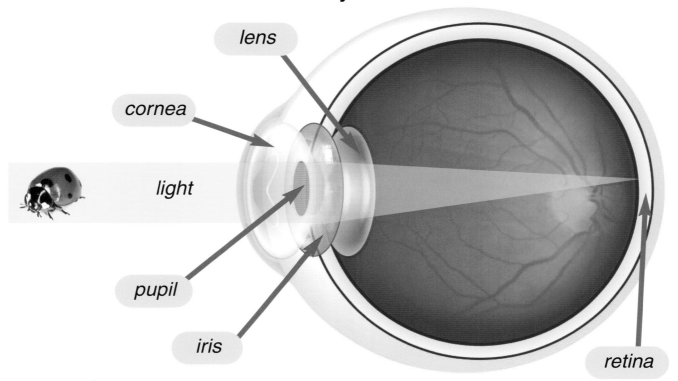

lens

cornea

light

pupil

iris

retina

Right to the retina

There are millions of light-sensitive nerves on each retina. The retina turns the light into messages. A special nerve, called the **optic nerve**, sends the messages from both eyes to your brain. Your brain then makes a picture of what you are looking at.

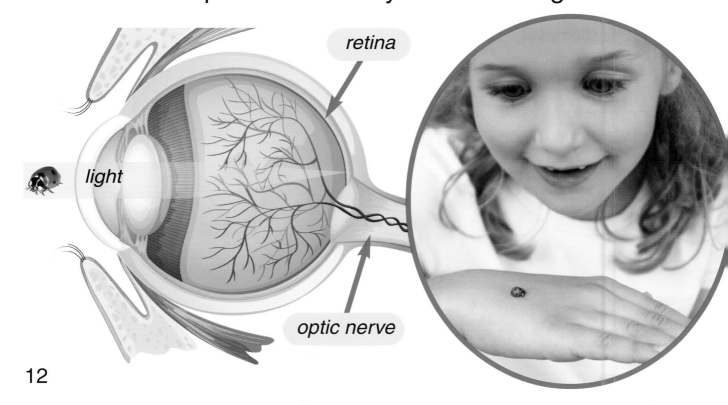

retina

light

optic nerve

Mixed-up messages

Sometimes your brain gets confused by the messages being sent by your eyes. Your brain makes a picture of an image that is different or is not really there. It is being tricked by an **optical illusion**. Optical illusions use light, color, or patterns to fool your brain. Some illusions can look very different to different people.

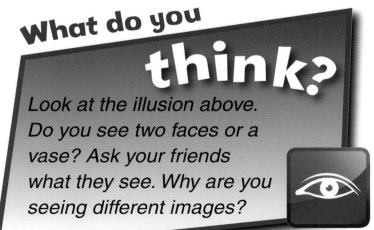

What do you think?

Look at the illusion above. Do you see two faces or a vase? Ask your friends what they see. Why are you seeing different images?

13

Lights out

It is difficult to see in the dark because there is very little light entering your eyes. Your pupils let light into your eyes. Each iris has many small muscles. They move to change the size of your pupils.

Letting in light

When you are somewhere with low light, your pupils get bigger. Bigger pupils let in more light to help you see. Too much light, however, can damage your retina. So, in bright light, your pupils get smaller. Smaller pupils only let in a little light.

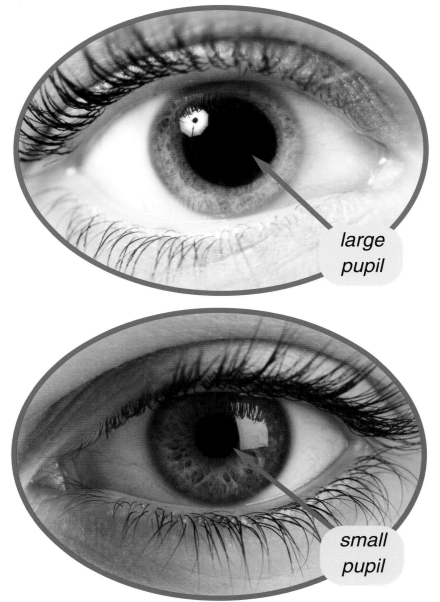

large pupil

small pupil

15

Animals see, too

Many animals can see much better than people. An eagle can spot its **prey** from more than one mile (1.6 km) away. Many animals, such as owls and cats, can see very well in the dark. Their pupils become very wide at night to let a lot of light into their eyes.

Different eyes

Giant squids have the largest eyes of any animal. Their eyes can be up to 10 inches (25 cm) in **diameter**! This allows them to see prey in the deep, dark ocean waters. A chameleon is a lizard that can move each eye separately. This means it can see in two different directions at the same time.

An insect's eyes can have thousands of tiny lenses.

Some spiders have up to eight eyes.

Help to see

Some people are **blind**. This means they cannot see anything at all. Some blind people have specially trained dogs that help them move around safely outside their homes. These dogs are called guide dogs.

What do you think?

How would you describe what the Moon looks like to someone who has never seen it before?

Wearing glasses

Sometimes people are born with damaged sight or they lose their sense of sight over time. These people may need glasses to help them see things clearly. Other people may have trouble telling the difference between certain colors. These people are color blind.

Some people wear glasses to see close up, others need help seeing far away.

Protect your eyes

It is important to protect your sense of sight. Very bright lights can damage your eyes. Never look directly at the Sun or at other very bright lights. On sunny days, be sure to wear sunglasses. Sunglasses protect your eyes from the bright Sun.

What do you think?

What is the difference between sunglasses and eyeglasses?

Take care of your eyes

If you are reading or doing homework, be sure there is enough light. Reading in dim, or low, light can strain your eyes. Take breaks to give your eyes a rest. Always keep sharp objects away from your eyes. Accidents with these objects can damage your eyesight.

See and draw

Going on a nature walk with an adult and some friends is a fun way to use your sense of sight. On the walk, look at the colors, shapes, and sizes of the things you see in nature. When you get home, draw a picture of all the things you saw on your walk. You will need:

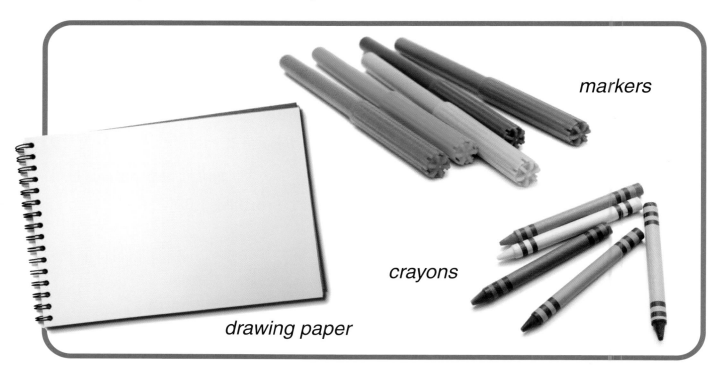

markers

crayons

drawing paper

22

Learning more

Books

What is Sight? (Lightning Bolt Books: Your Amazing Senses)
by Jennifer Boothroyd. Lerner Publications, 2009.

Look Here! (Let's Start Science) by Sally Hewitt.
Crabtree Publishing Company, 2008.

My Senses Help Me (My World) by Bobbie Kalman.
Crabtree Publishing Company, 2010.

Seeing (The Five Senses) by Rebecca Rissman.
Heinemann-Raintree, 2010.

Websites

Sightsavers—Kidzone—Eyes and seeing
www.sightsavers.org/kidzone/eyes-and-seeing/default.html

All About Your Senses: Experiments to Try
http://kidshealth.org/kid/closet/experiments/experiment_main.html

Sid the Science Kid
http://pbskids.org/sid/isense.html

The Sense of Sight
www.wisc-online.com/objects/ViewObject.aspx?ID=AP14304

Words to know

blind (blahynd) adjective Not able to see

cornea (KAWR-nee-uh) noun A clear covering over the eye

diameter (dahy-AM-i-ter) noun The width of a circle

iris (AHY-ris) noun The colored part of the eye

lens (lenz) noun Part of the eye that sends light to the retina at the back of the eye

optical illusion (OP-ti-kuhl ih-LOO-zhuhn) noun Something that tricks the brain into seeing something that is not real

optic nerve (OP-tik nurv) noun A long, thin nerve behind each eye; the optic nerve sends messages to the brain

prey (prey) noun Animals that are hunted and eaten by other animals

pupil (PYOO-puhl) noun The black center of the eye that lets in light

retina (RET-nuh) noun A thin lining on the back of each eye

A noun is a person, place, or thing. An adjective is a word that tells you what something is like.

Index

animals 16–17
blind 18
color blind 19
cornea 8, 10
glasses 19

iris 8, 9, 14
lens 8, 10, 11, 17
optic nerve 12
optical illusion 13
pupil 8, 9, 10, 14, 15, 16

retina 8, 11, 12, 15
safety 4, 5
senses 4, 5, 6, 7, 19, 20, 22

24